Crop Circles

by Carolyn North

RONIN
Berkeley, CA

Crop Circles

ISBN:1-57951-019-1
Copyright © 2001 Ronin Publishing, Inc.
Library of Congress Number   00-109766

Published by
RONIN Publishing, Inc.
PO Box 522, Berkeley, CA 94701
www.roninpub.com

KALEIDOSCOPE
FORMATION

Cover photograph: Steve Alexander
Cover design: Judy July, Generic Topography

Published in the United States of America
Printed by Bertelsmann
Distributed by Publishers Group West

Acknowledgements

For generously providing photographs, drawing, information and enthusiasm, I am grateful to Ruben Uriarte, Peter Sorensen, Freddie Silva, and Nancy Talbott; and to Ronin's publisher, Beverly Potter, for her vision. Special kudos to my husband, Herb Strauss, who is sure fast working pranksters with terrific night vision make the crop circles, but who lovingly supports me all the same.

—*Carolyn North*

WANING MOON
ROTATING EARTH

Silva

iii

EMERGING
STAR

Other Books

By Carolyn North

The Musicians and the Servants
A Novel of India

Seven Movements, One Song
Memoir as Metaphor

The Experience of a Lifetime
Living Fully, Dying Consciously

CIRCLE
TRIO

In the Beginning

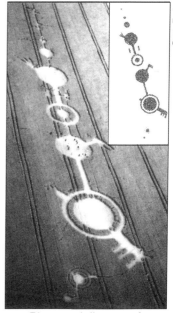

Busty Taylor

In the peak of summer, while boarding a bus in Cornwall for the southwest of England, a headline at the news agent's stand caught my eye:

Strange Formations Appear in Wiltshire Wheat Field

An aerial photograph showed a complex pictogram, eighty meters long, of ringed circles in a row sprouting lines and fingers—an ancient rune in wheat. I got on the bus. My destination, it just so happened, was Wiltshire.

Photo and diagram of Wiltshire pictogram.

This was not the first I had heard of "crop circles." Since the 1970s I had been following stories of unexplained circles showing up—overnight in most cases—in fields of oats, wheat, barley and oilseed rape.

Designs have appeared in sand, snow, trees, corn, sunflowers, and blueberries.

Some say reports of these circles go back even further than that. At the time I heard of them, circles were being reported mostly in the southwest counties of England, in the area surrounding Stonehenge and Avebury.

Perhaps it is coincidence, or perhaps not, that this area contains the highest concentration of prehistoric stone sites and earthworks in the world.

What are Crop Circles?

Crop circles are mysterious patterns first seen in wheatfields in the English countryside. Early circles were actually perfect ellipses in which the grain was in neat spirals with the stalks bent gently at a ninety degree angle to the ground.

Circles have appeared in grain at all stages of maturity. Amazingly, the grain was bent but not broken and continued to ripen healthily. The demarkation between a circle and the surrounding crop was always precise, as if cut by a cookie cutter. Except that not one stalk of grain was cut!

Circles appeared over-
night and were rarely seen
forming. Nobody had a
clue as to their origin.

History of a Mystery

In the 1970s and early 1980s, an occasional single crop circle appeared in one field or another, but in the summer of 1983 over thirty crop circles of varying circumferences and groupings showed up all over the countryside.

Between 1983 and 1986 the circles began to evolve in curious ways. In place of single circles, formations of circles occurred. Some were arranged in triangles, crosses, rows, mandalas. Some had inner concentric rings and single rings, others had double rings, some even had triple rings.

Crop **5** Circles

Single circle with swirled grain.

Crop **6** Circles

Carolyn North

Changing lay of wheat.

The lay of wheat, which in the early circles was laid straight down in a clockwise direction, now also ran counter-clockwise. In some formations the layers of wheat were interwoven; in some it lay in a spiral; in others it swept inward or outward from the center.

Glaser

Crop **7** Circles

Circles popping out in the English countryside were numbering into the hundreds each summer, their sizes increasing exponentially and their density increasing to up to thirty figures per ten acres. Some figures appeared on inaccessible slopes; others in full view of the road. The patterns of the smaller ones were visible from the ground, but the larger formations only made sense when seen from above. In every case the grain was bent but undamaged, with the rest of the field unaffected.

Glaser

CHICORA,
PENNSYLVANIA

By 1990, formations were appearing at the rate of five per night in England. Crop circles were also reported in Italy, Germany, Australia, Japan, Peru, Norway, Canada, Siberia, New Zealand and the United States. People were beginning to sit up and take notice. Researchers like Busty Taylor and Colin Andrews began to devote themselves full time to documenting the phenomenon.

Figures have evolved from single circles to intricate, complex works.

Pranksters Have Fun

Pranksters came onto the scene and tramped out some credible—but mostly incredible—designs. But they left the fields in a mess, broke the wheat stalks and made wobbly circles.

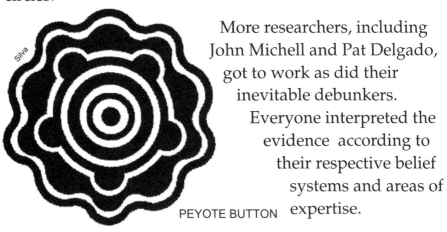

Silva

PEYOTE BUTTON

More researchers, including John Michell and Pat Delgado, got to work as did their inevitable debunkers. Everyone interpreted the evidence according to their respective belief systems and areas of expertise.

"Galloping hedgehogs, rutting deer...." claimed some, half tongue-in-cheek. "But why aren't the wheat stalks damaged?" we all wondered.

"The activity of earthworms weakening the roots; a virus; a fungus like fairy rings...," others claimed. "Ancient field markings, unexploded bombs from WWII, or the hole in the ozone layer...," claimed yet others.

"They're caused by stationary whirlwinds," exclaimed a meteorologist. But do whirlwinds create perfect cruciform figures?

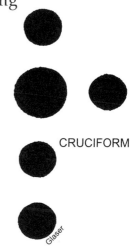

CRUCIFORM

Glaser

Glaser

"UFOs!" insisted others. "Sure, little green men," muttered the skeptics, while everyone nervously scanned the sky for the mysterious lights that had been reported by people who had never even heard of crop circles.

"Clearly," said some, "this is the work of clever hoaxsters." But could even the cleverest of hoaxsters create several designs a night in fields one hundred miles apart, and never once leave so much as a flashlight behind?

Designs made by hoaxsters are smaller, less complex and less symmetrical than those considered "genuine."

Nightfall in the northern latitudes occurs after 10:30 PM and dawn breaks by 5:00 AM. Consistently farmers tell of leaving their fields by dark, and returning at dawn to find a formation imprinted in their wheat, the field untrampled, the dew untouched upon the swirled stalks.

Investigations Begin

When complex pictograms suggestive of symbols from ancient mythologies and cultures—hieroglyphics, sacred geometry, runes—appeared in the formations, people from many disciplines began to investigate in earnest. Archeologists, art historians, linguists and medicine people came forth displaying similar patterns from the Celts, the Hopis of North America, the Australian aborigines. Tibetan thankas were found reflected in the wheat, petroglyphs from the Inuit.

Crop circles have been documented in 26 countries.

"If this is not a downright hoax," declared some meteorologists whose curiosity was aroused, "then we ought to be able to find a rational explanation for it."

Busty Taylor

Rune-like pictogram

Glaser

Crop **15** Circles

Electromagnetism was shown to move plants, but could neither bend nor flatten them. Stationary whirlwinds could create single circles, but nothing more intricate. Ball lightning generated microwaves in the atmosphere, but again was limited to the formation of questionable single circles.

Carolyn North

Fingers in the wheat.

Helicopter surveying a formation.

Investigations Aborted

More and more designs were popping up overnight in the wheatfields, and crop circle fever began taking over the English public, who traipsed out to the fields in droves. Tourists started to arrive from abroad. Army helicopters filled the air with their "choppers" as they looked for clues from above.

When a surveillance project was proposed by some of the more serious researchers, BBC TV and Nippon TV from Japan offered to support it with $2 million dollars worth of equipment. Even the British Army volunteered to participate. The plan was to observe an area often visited by crop circles, and to remain there for three weeks, monitoring and photographing the fields day and night. Shortly after all their equipment was set up, a circle appeared nearby. It was a clumsy hoax, believed by some to be perpetrated by those wishing to discredit the phenomenon, but the media gave it more publicity than all the circles together had received in a decade. The media investigators then packed up their equipment and left. The mystery was considered solved.

The hoax had the desired effect, for people could then shrug the whole thing off as a silly prank and not bother to think about it again. A few days later a beautiful formation—symmetrical, sharp-edged, wheat stalks unbroken—appeared imprinted in those same fields. By this time, however, only the committed researchers were watching.

Videographer Peter Sorensen recording a formation from a helicopter.

Mischievous Presence

WEST UNION,
OREGON

There is a prankish aspect to this crop circle mystery. More than once it has happened that someone has publicly expressed a wish to see some particular shape show up, only to find that shape imprinted in a nearby field shortly thereafter.

For example, when an atmospheric physicist wrote an article arguing that crop circles could be explained by an anomaly in wind patterns, his closing statement was "We shall soon have this phenomenon by the tail." A few days later, a circle appeared with a tail!

After he posited that in ringed circles the wheat always swirled in alternate directions, a new ringed circle appeared with wheat lying all in the same direction.

One cannot help but sense a mischievous presence which knows what we are thinking, teases us with these dazzlingly beautiful and complicated dis-plays, while coaxing us deeper and deeper into the mysteries of a labyrinth we may not have thought to go into before.

Japanese tourists meditated upon a specific design and it appeared within the week in a nearby field.

Some refuse to even look, some jump in with both feet running and others try to prove nothing unusual is happening in the first place.

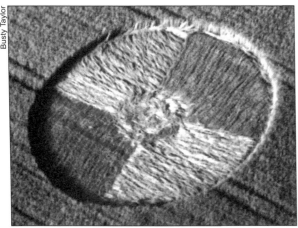
Ancient symbol of change.

When the whirl-wind theory which postulated that these mysterious ciclres were caused by stationary whirl-winds, was in its heyday, a magnificent circle appeared with four quadrants and an intricately woven hub. The wheat in each quadrant was swept neatly in different orientations, creating in textured pattern an ancient Celtic symbol indicating the coming of great changes. Four days later, as it happened, the Berlin Wall came down.

What's Going On Here?

By this time, nobody knew what to think. As one writer put it, "The circles began to multiply, the researchers began to divide and the historians began to despair." Occasional hoaxsters claimed the figures as their own. The media tried to ignore the phenomenon. The Army investigated secretly. Religious and environmental groups read messages of either hope or doom. Some people reported seeing balls of orange light over affected fields, and some people heard odd sounds.

Silva

SCORPION

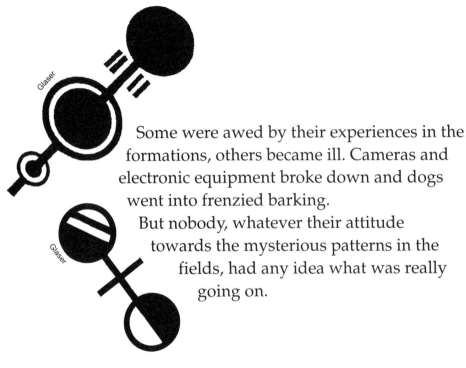

Some were awed by their experiences in the formations, others became ill. Cameras and electronic equipment broke down and dogs went into frenzied barking.

But nobody, whatever their attitude towards the mysterious patterns in the fields, had any idea what was really going on.

Reactions

Some farmers, outraged by the crowds appearing in their fields, harvested their crops immediately after a design appeared. Other farmers considered the formation a visitation and opened their fields to all who came, charging admission.

Circle in field being plowed.

Books and periodicals were printed; conferences were organized. This researcher and

Thousands of formations appear annually on every continent of the globe.

that researcher stopped speaking to each other. Advertisers used the circles in their ads and an innovative hairstyler even invented a "Crop Circle Cut."

My Day at a Pictogram

The day after I arrived in Wiltshire, I found my way to Alton Barnes in the Vale of Pewsey, the site of the pictogram in the newspaper. The terms "crop circle," "formation" and "design" were giving way to "pictogram"as the new forms became larger, more complex and more like pictorial works of art.

Carolyn North

People moved like colorful dots as they entered the mysterious formation in Wiltshire.

The day was hot, the air still and the grain almost ripe. The welcoming farm family, who was "hosting" the pictogram, sat beneath a striped umbrella by the roadside, charging a quid for entry and chatting companionably with the handful of us who had shown up at their quiet Wiltshire farm in the middle of the week.

Carolyn North

The curious exploring the formation.

An Army helicopter droned overhead, making circles in the air, and people moved like colorful dots along the narrow parallel tractor paths—called "tramlines"—to the pictogram in the center.

From the road, the design was recognizable only as a slight demarcation in the surface of the grain. To see the complex pattern, one had to get high above it, either on a nearby hillside or in an airplane—or walk into it along a tramline.

Ruben Uriarte

Tramlines

A person walking into a formation.

Carolyn North

I walked into the formation.

I paid my quid and with great anticipation, walked in.

Charged Atmosphere

I felt giddy. Was it just excitement at being there, or was I actually feeling the effect of the pictogram itself? Dowsers had reported strong responses from their rods and pendulums, and psychics claimed they felt powerful surges of energy - even years after the wheat had been harvested. I stood very still in the center of the first circle, closed my eyes and felt a definite wave of vertigo, which passed, leaving me quite lightheaded. Bubbly.

Carolyn North

A woman using a pendulum to dowse the circle.

In fact, everyone seemed bubbly. The atmosphere was light, as if we were all part of a great, warm-hearted joke. Strangers talked easily and bonded quickly, sharing viewpoints and wonderment.

People report feeling a "presence" as they walk in a crop circle.

A researcher interviewed each of us, while all the others listened. People held their pendulums, discussed earth energies, performed healings. It felt like being at a faire. We snapped pictures of each other and exchanged addresses, promising to connect up again in the city.

Not Alone

I circumambulated the largest circle, walking clockwise with the lay of the wheat and making a spiral into the center. I sensed a fullness in my throat, and an emotion which brought tears. My fingers tingled, and in my chest I felt a welling of gratitude. For what? The only words I can use to describe my state are that I knew I was not alone.

Not imagined

—I knew.

Grain outside Wiltshire formation.

Large rick-rack in Wiltshire formation.

Interwoven Grain

I tried to bend a stalk of wheat without breaking it, but it snapped in my fingers immediately.

"Look at this!" exclaimed one of my new friends, gently lifting the top layer of clockwise-swirled grain. The grain beneath that layer flowed counter-clockwise.

We carefully lifted the under-layer and found the next flow going clockwise. Beneath that, it again went counter clockwise! Between each layer where the wheat doubled back, the strands were neatly interwoven.

Inside the Wiltshire formation.

Just Listen

Pensive, I walked the whole figure slowly, paying attention to details in the design and subtle sensations in my body. Gradually, I grew calm and found myself smiling and deeply reassured. I felt in the presence of a benign intelligence with a sense of humor who had my interests at heart—a guide who wished only that we listen. Without a tick of hesitation, I agreed to listen to whatever it had to tell me, as I stepped into a hand-like figure that protruded from one of the smaller circles.

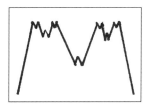

Each of the three fingers ended in a rick-rack design—like a massive M. But each point of the M was, in turn, rick-racked, and the points of each smaller M were rick-racked as well! To examine the detail, I knelt down, counting the number of stalks left standing between each of the smallest points. There were nine—exactly—*in each one.* Although the day was hot, I shivered.

Carolyn North

Rick-rack design in edge of formation.

Increasing Complexity

The growing season of 1991 brought pictograms—by this time also referred to as glyphs and agriglyphs—by the hundreds. Many now resembled segmented creatures, sea creatures. It was as

Silva

if the circle-makers—whoever or *whatever* they might be—were perfecting their techniques, variations on each theme appeared in field after field all over England.

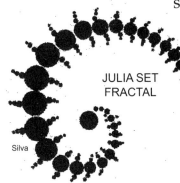

JULIA SET FRACTAL

Silva

Circles, lines, squiggles, ladders, keys showed up in every imaginable configuration.

High Art

And then, just before the end
of the season, we were all
stunned by the appear-
ance of two gorgeous
works of art that had no
precedents in any of the
glyphs that had been seen to date.

BARBARY CASTLE
FORMATION

Glaser

One, near Barbary Castle in Wiltshire,
was a huge equilateral triangle with a double-
ringed circle, each angle sprouting a circular
formation. Some called it a three-dimensional
tetrahedron. Its proportions, we later learned, were
perfect.

The other, not far from the Mathematics Department at England's Cambridge University, was a close-to perfect representation of the Mandelbrot Set which is a computer-generated configuration known as a "fractal." In a fractal the proportions of a figure are the same no matter how much it is reduced or magnified—and it was the size of a football stadium!

Both formations were breathtakingly beautiful. Both were enormous. Both had appeared overnight and neither could be explained by any theory that had been posited before.

MANDELBROT
SET FRACTAL

Glaser

Enter Doug and Dave

Late in the 1992 growing season in England, Doug Brower and Dave Chorley, two buddies in their sixties "confessed" that they dreamed up the circles as a joke in the pub one night. For thirteen years they said they tromped out all the circles in the night using only a few planks and some string.

Swirled grain figures have a textured pattern of wave-like crests not producible by human feet tromping on planks.

The media grabbed the story and gave it coverage all over the world—before watching Doug and Dave demonstrate, quite clearly, that all they could do was make an unconvincing mess of broken grain. But the story was out, and it was too late to retract it even if the media had wanted to.

I first heard of Doug and Dave when they showed up on the local TV news, and found it hard to put their blustering bravado together with the pristine brilliance of either the ringed triangle or the complex fractal. I was immediately on my guard. But even though I wasn't ready to be convinced, the general public apparently was, which, I suspected, was the point of the exercise.

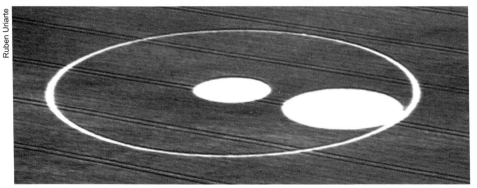

Ruben Uriarte

Circles within a circle.

Media Silence

"Didn't two guys do it?" one still hears when the subject comes up. In the years since their confession much of the Western media has been silent on the subject, even though new formations appearing in Japan receive front-page coverage in Japanese newspapers.

ALBERTA, CANADA
Silva

After several farmers threatened to sue Doug and Dave for wanton destruction of their crops, the duo admitted to doing "about a dozen." They claimed to have retired from their circlemaking activities. Since then, one has died, and circles have appeared with delicate rings only inches wide in which a man's foot wouldn't have fit anyway.

SASKATCHEWAN

Nonetheless the formations continue to appear in ever greater complexity in cultivated crops all over the world—in sunflowers in Germany, in sugarcane in Mexico, in blueberries in Maryland!

Motives

PENNSYLVANIA

One cannot help but wonder about Doug and Dave's motives. As C.G. Jung said, there are changes happening in the collective psyche in this Millennial time. There are those who might well fear the inevitable changes, especially those in positions of power. The challenge to the existing institutions of state, religion, science and economy are implicit in a happening for which there is no "natural" explanation.

The reaction of a terrified populace could well create uncontrollable mayhem. So a campaign of disinformation, including the possible hiring of adventurers to create credible pictograms, and the presence of information seekers amongst the crop circle organizations was not too surprising a response.

Laughingstock

The community of researchers was at the mercy of the public's mocking attention—humiliated and wary. Nevertheless, pictograms continued to appear all over the world.

Ruben Uriarte

Formation with Sanscrit letter in the center.

The public, to the extent they knew of the formations at all, assumed they were made by "the two guys who confessed" or copy-catters out on a lark.

Doug and Dave have been out of the picture since the early 90s, yet circles keep appearing in increasing complexity.

In fact, many were. Serious researchers think that about 20% of the designs showing up in England each year are made by human artists—some quite skillfully—or by people sincerely attempting to communicate back to the circlemakers.

The researchers grew disheartened, under the pressure of public mockery, internal disagreements, and racing around the country only to discover another hoax. The whole subject went underground for a few years, and people stopped paying attention.

Still They Appear

Pictograms have appeared in sand in Egypt, in snow in Turkey. They showed up in barley in Czecheslovakia, in wheat in Ohio, in rice in Japan. One formation was reported in oats just outside the city limits of New York City.

CHEHALIS, WASHINGTON

Silva

While the media was silent, public curiosity all but nonexistent and researchers still licking their wounds, the pictograms continued to appear, larger— up to 2500 feet long! —and more beautiful than before.

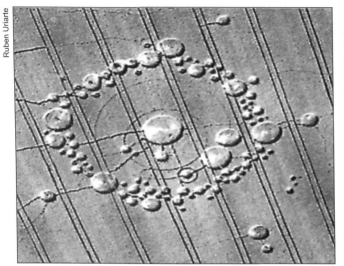

Ruben Uriarte

Asteroids depicted by circlemakers.

Safe from the hordes of curiosity seekers who had lost interest, the circlemakers gave us galaxy formations, joined crescents, Sanscrit letters and complex geometries all on the grand scale. The real mystery was that except for a few diehard researchers, these marvelous works of art were being ignored!

For a few years even I was not paying attention. But foolishly, I now believe, for had they been done by gifted hoaxsters in England, or been copy-catted around the world by many discreet artists who left neither heelprints nor a

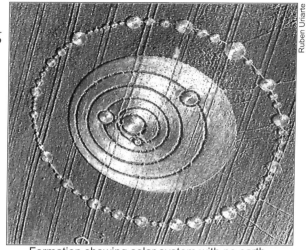

Formation showing solar system with no earth.

demand for recognition in their wake, would the phenomenon be any the less remarkable?

Unidentified Lights, Sounds, Crafts

Silva

LITTLEBURY
BLOSSOM

From every part of the globe come reports of strange luminous objects seen hovering in the neighborhoods of affected fields. They have been described as bright lights—red, orange, purplish, yellow, white. People have described "crafts" which appear, stop in the air, and then disappear. Balls of light were seen to flash, circle, drop from nowhere. One moment they are there and the next moment they are gone.

Silva

Sometimes these sightings have been accompanied by chirping, buzzing or roaring sounds, and sometimes they were silent. Lights have been captured on film, sounds recorded on tape recorders and people have been increasingly more willing to tell of their experiences which range from simple sightings to tales of abduction and memory loss.

RIBBON
WREATH

With the "impossible" being experienced by people all over the world, and the general public lulled into ignoring what would not fit the mainstream mindset, it became imperative to do scientific studies on the affected grain, as well as to   examine the soil beneath the roots, the groundwater beneath the figures and the radioactivity within the sites.

Enter the Mathematicians

More recent seasons have featured pictograms resembling natural forms such as double helixes, DNA, asteroid belts, spiral nebulae, galaxies, eclipses and moon phases. It was as if the circlemakers were trying to get the attention of the scientific community. Although many scientists continued to show little interest—often belligerently so—others were curious enough to buck their colleagues' judgments and, without official funding, take a careful look at the geometry and proportions of the formations.

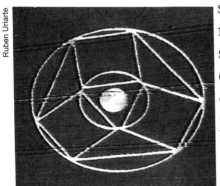

Geometric figure in grain.

Painstakingly measuring the proportions of multi-circle figures, the mathematician Gerald Hawkins found that their numbers corresponded to the ratios of the diatonic scale—the eight note octave on the white keys of the piano. Pictograms in later years, as well as containing these same diatonic ratios, were found to be constructed upon one basic geometric figure.

DIATONIC SCALE

Several formations seemed to illustrate four new theorems of Euclidian Geometry that were hinted at, but not actually present in Euclid's own works!

Silva

Curiously, the eight-note octave sound occurs naturally only in bird and whale song. For the designs to authenticate these diatonic ratios, the measurements of the formations had to be accurate to within inches! And they were.

Research

Observers photographed and scientists began sampling, measuring, and analyzing data gleaned from the fields. Foremost among the researchers is the BLT Research Team formed in 1989, consisting of John Burke, William Levengood and Nancy Talbott, headquartered in Cambridge, Massachusetts. They have been examining plant and soil samples collected from all over the world by hundreds of re-searchers from inside crop formations, from the surrounding crop nearby, and from totally unaffected fields.

Following strict scientific protocol, BLT Team researchers discovered a consistent pattern of alterations in the mysteriously constructed circles, but not in formations made by people, or in the surrounding, unaffected fields. Here's what they found:

Microwave radiation may be the force used to create the formations.

Plant Stems

The nodes—the knotty "joints" on the plant stems—are affected in two ways depending upon the plant's maturity. When a crop formation occurs in pliable, young plants the nodes are elongated—sometimes as much as 200%—as if they had been blasted by a heat source which has evaporated the moisture in the plant stem, producing steam which has stretched the nodes lengthwise.

Nodes of grain stalk from outside of crop circles are unaffected.

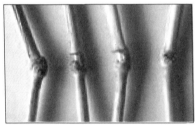

Nodes of grain stalk from inside a crop circle have expanded and lengthened.

In more mature crop, which has tougher outer fibers, the steam tends to explode the nodes, leaving expulsion cavities or small blown-out craters at the nodes.

In some crop formations the node length changes are greatest at the center, with the changes decreasing towards the edge of the flattened circle. This linear decrease fits with the Beer-Lambert Principle—a law in physics that describes how matter absorbs electromagnetic energy. The correlation, which approaches .97, clearly rules out the plank and board theory.

Further, standing stalks within a crop formations are often found to have node length changes as great, or nearly as great, as the downed crop. In some cases, node length changes are found in standing crop outside the flattened areas.

The BLT team findings rule out the plank and board theory.

About their findings, Nancy Talbott asks rhetorically, "How can manual flattening of plants account for this?

Seeds

Under the microscope, enlarged cell wall pits have been observed in the bract tissue, the thin membrane which surrounds the seed heads through which nutrients pass to the developing seeds. When crop formations occur in young crop, the seed heads are found to be empty of seeds or the seeds are stunted which, exhibit massively repressed growth and other abnormalities, when germinated.

In mature crop, seeds are small, but germinate five times as quickly as in unaffected grain.

What is especially remarkable, however, is that when a formation occurs in more mature crop the seed are "energized" so that they germinate and grow at up to five times the normal rate and size with more produce.

The BLT Team is exploring agricultural application of their findings. Could it be that knowledge gained from their study of crop circles will teach us how to increase crop production?

DNA LOOK-A-LIKE

Silva

Soil

Expected concentrations of magnetic particles of meteoritic iron is 0.4 mg. per gram of soil. But BLT found crop circle soils to have considerably higher concentration of iron particles. These magnetic particles are microscopic in size—50-100 microns in diameter. When analyzed with electron dispersive spectroscopy, the particles are found to be pure iron. Talbott says the rounded shape and tiny size indicates they have fallen to earth in a molten state further pointing to the presence of microwave radiation.

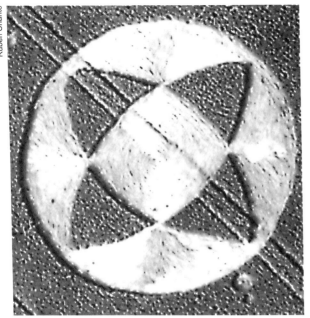

Four-fold geometry.

In some cases the magnetic particles are concentrated more heavily at the edge of the formation than in the center. BLT Research Team biophysicist Levengood's calculations indicate that the particles have been flung out by centrifugal force.

Anomolous deposits of a white powdery or gelatinous substance are occasionally found inside crop formations. BLT's preliminary laboratory analysis of these materials indicates very unusual purity levels of silicon or silicon compounds.

Findings by Lay Researchers

Freddie Silva is exploring the relationship of sound to the designs. Michael Glickman and Patricia Murray are analyzing the geometry of the figures. Ruben Uriarte is researching the formations in Mexico and South America. Others, including Linda Mouton Howe, Lucy Pringle, Iiyes, Karen Douglas, gather and sift evidence and pose provocative questions.

Glaser

Much of this work has been aided by the remarkable video photography of Peter Sorenson, who *Time Magazine* featured on its as cover "croppie" of the year, and by the amazing photographs of Steven Alexander and Busty Taylor.

Ruben Uirte

Nine-fold geometry.

Croppies, as crop circle researchers are affectionately called, sometimes find charring at the Y-junctures of lines in a formation, but only at the outer epidermal layer. The cellular structure beneath is not burned, suggesting a heat source that is brief and rapidly applied.

Groundwater

Aerial photographs taken with infra-red film show the drying up of groundwater beneath the site formations that persists for several days to a week, before the water table returns to normal. In human-made designs, there are no changes in groundwater.

Ground water beneath formations is temporarily depleted.

Animals

Spider web

Occasionally, insects or small rodents are found dead in and amongst the downed crop. Sometimes formations are dotted with dead flies still clinging to the seed heads, while the standing crop outside the figure have no clinging dead flies.

In Canada, geese flying in a V formation were observed to split into two groups to fly around, rather than over, a crop circle.

Anomalies

Many researchers, including the BLT team, have reported that electronic equipment often dysfunctions at the site of a formation, sometimes continuing to do so long after the crop has been harvested. Cameras, recording devices and cell phones have been reported to stop working inside formations and resume functioning when placed outside the design. Compasses in airplanes flying above a site have been found to go awry.

A Geiger counter measuring radioactivity inside one formation found the microsievert/hour number to be elevated from 0.13 microsievert/hour to 0.38 microsievert/hour.

RADIATING PARTICALS?

Silva

Humans

Preliminary studies by Lucy Pringle of the effects of crop circles on people indicate that exposure to the formations seems to affect the endocrine system, increasing hormone levels in the pineal, thyroid and pituitary glands. In some cases post-menopausal women visiting the formations have been known to start their menses again!

JULIAN SET
FRACTAL

Silva

These changes suggest that an energetic system of intense heat and force—like the energy contained in solar flares—occurring in extremely brief, precisely aimed bursts is what physically causes the phenomenon.

The BLT team has isolated an electrical force, previously unrecorded by scientists, that they call plasma disturbances which they believe is central to creating certain of the plant changes. But who—or what—has delivered it? What is it and how is it happening? Why now? Nobody knows.

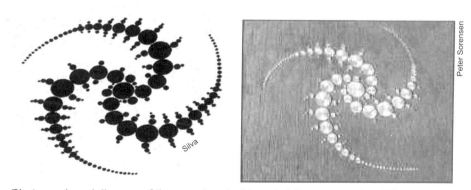

Photograph and diagram of the amazing double spiral that appeared on Windmill Hill.

Snowflake fractal woven into grain.

Mysterious Masterpieces

Over the years, figures containing three, four and five geometric segments evolved to figures with seven and then

ten-fold geometries. Fractals appeared in varying shapes, often with complicated outlines of small circles numbering into the hundreds.

The circlemakers used more textures, creating subtle shadings in the downed grain by sweeping it in varying directions to catch light and shadow as the sun moved across the sky.

Textured seven-fold geometry.

They left standing tufts of grain at perfectly spaced intervals, creating a dappled effect; they swirled the grain into standing "nests;" they repeated curves and scallops, creating a sense of motion.

Grain swirled into a nest.

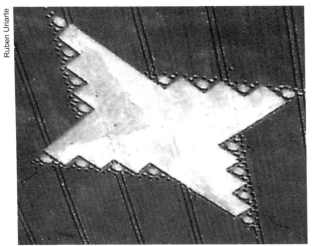

Aztec in grain.

The subtle internal patterns made some designs appear three dimensional, causing flat fields to look like cubes and pyramids and writhing serpents. Optical illusions of many sorts tricked the

eye, making us laugh with surprise. New pictograms that were gorgeous but simply "ordinary" began to seem ho-hum.

The Magic Basket

In the growing season just before the turning of the Millenium, a huge mandala appeared that was *actually* three-dimensional! It contained standing tufts of grain and textured lays, as well as woven expanses of grain, like a loosely constructed basket which rose up from the ground in a graceful weave.

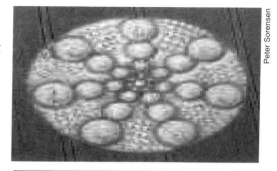

Peter Sorensen

The Magic Basket

Fortunately, it was discovered by one researcher/photographer flying overhead early that morning because when the farmer discovered it he mowed it down before the public could descend on his fields. Of this stunning and remarkable three-dimensional "basket," we have only one tantalizing photograph.

Eyewitnesses

Over the years there have been a few eyewitnesses to the actual moments of a formation's appearance. People have reported seeing balls of light in the sky, heard strange sounds and seen portions of crop suddenly flatten to the ground. In Romania, one farmer relates hearing a "terrible whistling sound and a wind so ferocious it tore the hat off my head and flung me to the ground."

In the Netherlands, for example, there is a farm in Hoeven in which crop circles have appeared several times each growing season, sometimes two or more simultaneously. The farmer's son witnessed several circles, which were mostly simple, single designs, as they have formed.

Tree circles have appeared in Canada and Czecheslovakia, the trunks bent but not broken.

He said that at first he heard a crackling noise, looked up and saw a stationary ball of light hovering about twelve feet over the field. After about twenty seconds the light faded, but just before it went out, a section of the field corkscrewed and whooshed down into a neat design in seconds.

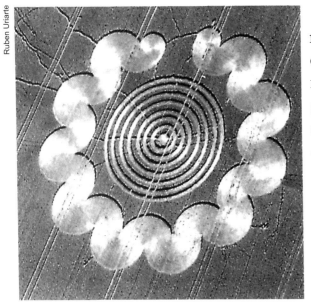

Ruben Uriarte

Scallops and Squiggles.

It felt like being near an electrical outlet, he said. He reported that the ground immediately afterwards was almost too hot to touch. Some 70 witnesses interviewed by researcher Colin Andrews, all claimed that it took only seconds for the design they witnessed to form.

Amazingly, long after the fields have been harvested, when winter snows cover the exposed soils, the contours of circles re-appear by melting the snow where crop circles have been to reveal the same exact formation.

What's Going on?

If one perceives the "real" world as being limited to what humans and their instruments can see, hear, or measure, then a phenomenon like crop circles is either explainable by "natural" causes, or it is impossible to exist.

JULIA SET
FRACTAL

MARRIAGE OF THE
MOON AND THE SUN

And if it is "impossible" but there it is anyway, then what are our options to explain it? Either we can refuse to deal with it, or we can open our minds to strange, new possibilities.

If, on the other hand, one perceives the world as an intelligent composite of interlocking dimensions—the visible and the invisible—then anything we can imagine, and much that we cannot imagine, is potentially possible. Thus, some "something" we do not understand might conceivably coexist with us as a part of the universe we have not yet experienced. Have not microscopes and telescopes, over the years, revealed to us all manner of things we assumed were not there because we could not see them?

Getting Attention

Perhaps the crop circles are a means of catching our attention. They do, after all, stimulate us to debate about them, forcing us to discard one explanation after another until we are brought up short against the wall of our understanding. Confused and exhausted, we may finally just stop and, letting go of everything we know, simply listen.

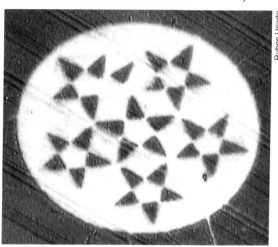

Ruben Uriarte

Pentacles in grain—with one opened.

Listening, we might begin to hear that there exist intelligent forces beyond our rational means of understanding that are capable of moving dense matter and creating, for our edification, these remarkable, impermanent works of art.

Ruben Uriarte

Cat's eyes near Liddington castle.

Sacred Art

What I find reassuring is that this mysterious force seems to care enough about our welfare and the welfare of our planet to go to the trouble of sending us these communications, which in their beauty and amazing complexity seem to indicate that we are sacred beings living in a sacred universe where marvelous things can and do happen.

For I believe the pictograms in the fields are indeed sacred art. Like all great art they resonate with us at our deepest levels where we connect with all existence, seen and unseen. The formations suggest, in their

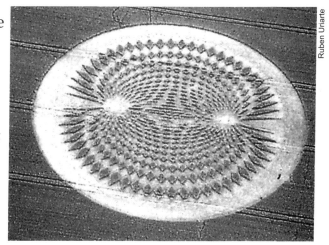

Ruben Uriarte

Electro-magnetic morie.

form and proportions, a many-layered, multi-dimensional web of meaning, reflecting the connected, glorious net that makes up the Universe itself.

Ruben Uriarte

Dolphins in Barbury Castle Crescents.

Cosmic Order

When I look at a figure like the Barbary Castle formation, in which the central circle contained *exactly* the combined areas of the circles around it; or the stunning double spiral on Windmill Hill which was 1000 feet long and contained 194 separate circles, I feel profoundly moved by their perfection, as if I am in the presence of some higher cosmic intelligence which is communicating with me.

The proportions and symmetry of the designs evoke in me a sense of universal order, as if their proportions and my proportions were in harmony. Looking at them, I see myself mirrored, and I see myself Whole.

Stacked Functions

I expect that each human reaction to
these masterpieces in the fields contains
part of the truth - from stationary
whirlwinds to unseen intelligences—
and I wonder if the evoking of a human
response is not one aspect of its purpose.

I wonder if its purposes are not multiple and that we
are being addressed on many levels simultaneously, from the
physical to the spiritual. In the language of Permaculture,
which is a design system for creating sustainable human, plant
and animal environments, this is called "Stacked Functions"
which means that the crop circles are significant in a multiplic-
ity of ways—probably in more ways than we can imagine.

Their designs, their energy, their geometry, their placement, their sequence, their genetic changes etc. may all serve to enliven the planet in one way or another. This could mean that everybody who has a hypothesis is partly correct, and that we need everone's insights to get to the truth of these mysterious artworks.I believe the crop circles are here for a reason, and that reason may have to do with guiding us through the great changes that are before us.

RubenUriarte

Five-fold pinwheel.

World Change

During every major world change in the past, great teachers have appeared to guide humanity into a new stage of conscious- ness. It

Three dimensional woven ribbon near Bechhampton.

Ruben Uriarte

Glaser

seems to be time again. The old consciousness no longer works so well for us; the fit is tight and we are choking—ourselves and our planet.

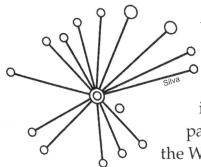

As I gaze at these beautiful formations in the crops, I see whole systems, every part in relation to every other part, the Whole forming a thing of beauty. Like us, the parts do not exist independently of the Whole. *Wholeness*, I feel, is what is sacred, and the sacred includes everything in the world. This vast everything—dark and light, good and evil—is in constant flux, nothing separate from anything else, nothing outside the Whole. It is like a wheel of many dimensions—a living, breathing, conscious wheel.

LAGUNA CANYON
CALIFORNIA

SANTA ROSA
CALIFORNIA

Staff of Life

It seems significant that crop circles are appearing primarily in grains, the staff of life. In the staple food crops of every corner of the world—wheat, corn, oats, barley, rice, soybean, millet—these mysterious designs are not only beautiful but also of enhanced nutritive value, as the BLT team has discovered.

Hunger is rampant in the world and our societies and economies know little about sharing. Children starve and sicken while nations stockpile food until it rots while we are helpless to do anything about it.

Carolyn North

Staff of life.

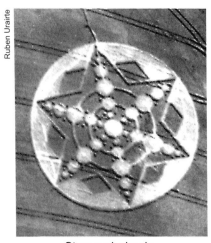

Stars and wheels.

As a species we seem to have lost our way. There are great changes afoot which are compatible with the end of an era, as Jung said, and we seem to be scrambling blindly on a dark road, frightened and defensive, not knowing which way to turn.

Fouling the nest of the earth, starving and murdering our siblings, neglecting our young, we have forgotten why we are here. Our structures and institutions are in trouble, our systems barely serve our collective needs and our environment—the source of our lives—is under seige.

We are out of balance now. The center will not hold. As we search the skies for other intelligent life in the universe, doesn't it make sense that other intelligent life in the universe may be responding to us? Perhaps we are not the only ones who know that the issue is urgent and that it's time for a shift to happen.

Trinity in circles.

Where next?

Circles of stones have appeared in Puerto Rico. In Czechoslo-
vakia, a leafy circle of trees bent inward at the base but
otherwise was unbroken. Up to 2000 designs have been
reported in India since 1986. In England, on one summer
night 5 formations appeared simultaneously!

They are Everywhere

Perhaps we'll soon be finding crop circles in our own back-
yards. Might they be urging us to wake up, take notice and
save ourselves and our planet before it's too late? I would
like to think so. They seem to be demonstrating that the
crisis we are in need not lead to depression, but that the way
can be beautiful and innovative and playful.

I'm Ready

Personally, I'm ready for some of the creative fun which leaps over fences, erases shopworn definitions, cuts huge swaths in the fields of the world and stuns everyone around with mind-boggling beauty.

All it takes is opening my mind, taking a deep breath and making that first, grand leap!

Dynamic torus.

About the Author

Carolyn North is an author interested in earth energies, works as a healer using movement and sound, and is a social activist doing what she can to

Carolyn (right) and friend in a crop circle.

restore balance and wholeness on the individual, community and planetary levels. She is the founder of "The Daily Bread Project" which gathers surplus food and delivers it to agencies that serve the hungry.

"Although I appear to have a finger in many pies, to me they are one pie."

Mother of three children, she lives with her husband, a University of California Chemistry professor , in Berkeley, Ca.

Contact Information

The BLT Team offers a packet of information on their research for a modest fee and is seeking field workers. To inquire or report a formtion contact: BLT Research Team, Inc., Box 40127, Cambridge, MA 02140, Ph 617/492-0415, Fax 617/492-0414.

- **Steve Alexander** is an award winning photographer/author, and offers postcards and calendars, http://cropcircleconnector.com/temporarytemple/library, temporarytemples@netscapeonline.co.uk.
- **Freddie Silva** is a researcher/lecturer, offers posters and articles, http://home.clara.net/lovely/crop_circles_art.html.
- **Peter Sorensen** is a videographer and was featured on the Cover of *Time Magazine* as "Croppie of the Year," http://cropcircleconnector.com/Sorensen/Peter/Sorensen99.html.
- **Busty Taylor** is a researcher/photographer and organizes conferences, www.aviation-uk.com/copper/98busty2.htm.
- **Ruben Uriarte** is North California MUFON Director and leads tours abroad. www.beyondboundries.org, ruben_uriarte@hotmail.com, 510/489-3686.